Community Helpers

Principals

by Erika S. Manley

Bullfrog Books

Ideas for Parents and Teachers

Bullfrog Books let children practice reading informational text at the earliest reading levels. Repetition, familiar words, and photo labels support early readers.

Before Reading

- Discuss the cover photo. What does it tell them?
- Look at the picture glossary together. Read and discuss the words.

Read the Book

- "Walk" through the book and look at the photos. Let the child ask questions. Point out the photo labels.
- Read the book to the child, or have him or her read independently.

After Reading

- Prompt the child to think more. Ask: Have you met your school's principal? What do you like about his or her job?

Bullfrog Books are published by Jump!
5357 Penn Avenue South
Minneapolis, MN 55419
www.jumplibrary.com

Library of Congress Cataloging-in-Publication Data

Names: Manley, Erika S., author.
Title: Principals / by Erika S. Manley.
Description: Minneapolis, MN: Bullfrog Books are published by Jump!, [2020]
Series: Community helpers
Audience: Grades: K to Grade 3.
Audience: Ages: 5–8. | Includes index.
Identifiers: LCCN 2018058171 (print)
LCCN 2018061063 (ebook)
ISBN 9781641288392 (ebook)
ISBN 9781641288378 (hardcover : alk. paper)
ISBN 9781641288385 (paperback)
Subjects: LCSH: School principals—Juvenile literature.
Classification: LCC LB2831.9 (ebook)
LCC LB2831.9 .M35 2020 (print)
DDC 371.2/012—dc23 LC record available at https://lccn.loc.gov/2018058171

Editor: Jenna Trnka
Designer: Shoreline Publishing Group

Photo Credits: Mypicksy/iStock, cover (left); Steve Debenport/iStock, cover (right), 14–15; SolStock/iStock, 1, 19, 23br; Pictac/iStock, 3; imtmphoto/Shutterstock, 4; alseeit/iStock, 5, 23bl; michaeljung/Shutterstock, 6–7; FatCamera/iStock, 8, 16–17; Sean Locke Photography/Shutterstock, 9, 23tr; Africa Studio/Shutterstock, 10–11; DGLImages/iStock, 12–13; a_v_d/Shutterstock, 18; Kali9/iStock, 20–21; monkeybusinessimages/iStock, 22; wavebreakmedia/Shutterstock, 23tl; Rob1713/Dreamstime, 24.

Printed in the United States of America at Corporate Graphics in North Mankato, Minnesota.

Table of Contents

School Leaders

Lucy wants to be a principal.

What do they do?

They lead
the school.

They lead
teachers.

They lead
us, too!

Mom takes me to school.

Pam greets me!

classroom

Fred used to be a teacher.

He knows what
we need to learn.

He helps us in
the classroom!

Kim meets with teachers.

She listens to them.

Why?

To help them
with problems.

family

Sam meets with Lon's family.

Why?

Lon is being bullied.

Sam will help keep Lon safe.

Kia visits our class.

She builds with us.

Cool!

It is time for recess.

Principal Lin plays!

Fun!

Principals are our friends!

At the Principal's Office

office
The principal works in the entire school, but his or her office is where the principal meets with students and their family members. It can be a private place for talking.

desk
The principal does work at his or her desk.

Picture Glossary

bullied
Treated in a cruel, insulting, or threatening way.

greets
Meets and welcomes.

principal
The head of a school.

recess
A break from schoolwork.

Index

To Learn More

Finding more information is as easy as 1, 2, 3.

1. Go to www.factsurfer.com
2. Enter "principals" into the search box.
3. Choose your book to see a list of websites.

FACT SURFER